ASPECTS OF GREEK L

MINOAN CR

ELIZABETH McLELLAN

Principal teacher of Classics,
Cleveden Secondary School, Glasgow

LONGMAN

1: THE FORGOTTEN LAND

Homer's Crete

In the middle of the wine-dark sea there lies a land called Crete . . . a rich and lovely land, washed by the waves on every side. Many people live there—so many that they cannot be counted.

There are 90 cities on the island and each one has its own language. One of the 90 is a great city called Knossos. There, for nine years, King Minos ruled, and was specially dear to Zeus.

Homer *Odyssey* Book XIX

Crete lies in the Eastern Mediterranean

That description of the island of Crete, in the Eastern Mediterranean, was made in about 800 BC by the Greek poet Homer. Homer was not speaking about the island as he knew it, but as it had been 700 years before. When Homer knew it, there were only the ruins of the island's splendid cities left. Knossos, the city of King Minos, and his great palace could no longer be seen. There was no trace of Minos or of his people (sometimes called the Minoans after their King). Ships trading in the Mediterranean passed by the island of Crete.

But King Minos still lived in legend. Every Greek, since his childhood, had heard stories of Zeus, Father of the Gods, and how Zeus visited the Earth and made men and women his friends. Minos, King of Crete was one of his special friends.

The ruins of the Palace at Knossos

An ancient Cretan ship. The sails have been drawn so clearly that you can easily see how the weave makes a pattern on them.

How Knossos was destroyed

We know that Crete, and the site of Knossos itself, lies in the centre of an earthquake area. Not far from Crete, about 110 kilometres to the north, lies the island of **Thera**, now called Santorini. You can see it on the map. This tiny island may give us a clue to the disappearance of King Minos and his kingdom.

Thera is a volcanic island. Its volcano last erupted in 1941, and before that in 1925. There have been many other eruptions, one of which was 3,500 years ago, in about 1500 BC. It was so violent that it left a vast crater on the island itself. At that time Knossos and King Minos were still rich and powerful. People think that a tidal wave, followed by an earthquake and then a fire, caused by the eruption of the volcano on Thera, may have destroyed Knossos.[1] In the following pages you will read why people think this.

[1] This is one current theory but not everyone believes it. Some people think the eruption on Thera may have been 400 years earlier.

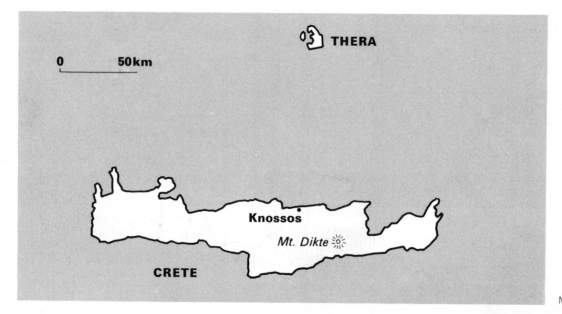

Map showing Thera in relation to Crete

Thera, now called Santorini, with its great crater filled by the sea.

This photograph was taken when Thera erupted in 1925

Earthquake, flood and fire

We do not know what that terrible eruption of Thera, 3,500 years ago, was really like. Few people in those days could write, and no one took the trouble to write down the story of what had happened. But we do know what more recent volcanic eruptions have been like.

In the drawing you can see how a volcano erupts. Tremendous underground heat, and pressure from above, melts the solid rock. Then the molten rock is forced right up the central passage, until it bursts out at the top. You can imagine how violently this happens and how terrifying it must be to see and hear.

Showers of ash are hurled up into the air, and cover the countryside for miles around. When a volcanic island erupts, great walls of water sweep violently across the sea. These are called **tidal waves**.

People who have seen eruptions say that one of the most frightening things is the noise. The volcano roars and bellows like an angry bull.

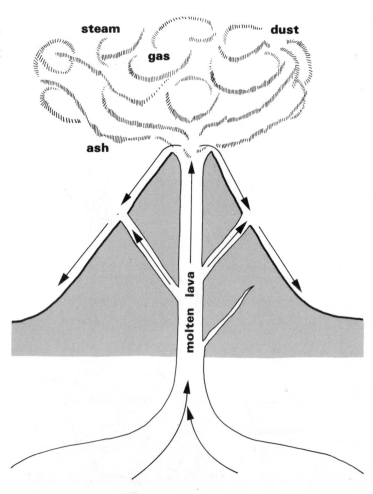

A volcano erupts

An eruption that we know about from books and photographs took place in 1883 on the volcanic island of **Krakatoa** in the Pacific. The volcano began to erupt in May 1883. A huge column of dust rose high into the air and could be seen for miles around. The noise of the explosion could be heard 160 kilometres away.

At last, late in August, the volcano finally exploded. Darkness like the darkest night spread far around. The crew of a ship close to the island reported seeing 'one second intense blackness, the next a blaze of fire'.

The eruption was so violent and dramatic that part of the island itself was flung into the air. When people finally thought it safe to go near the island, they found that part of it had disappeared.

Vibrations from this eruption caused ruin and destruction in places as far as 160 kilometres from Krakatoa. Tidal waves rushed across the sea, and walls of water more than 15 metres high flooded towns and villages. Over 30,000 people drowned.

Krakatoa after the eruption in 1883. Compare with the picture on page 5

It is easy to believe that the eruption of Thera in 1500 BC must have been like the eruption of Krakatoa. Certainly the tidal wave could easily have travelled the 110 kilometres from Thera to Crete.

People knew that the great civilisation of King Minos of Crete had been suddenly and violently destroyed, but no one knew how. Then, after Krakatoa erupted, people thought about Thera and remembered the eruption 3,500 years before. Once they noticed how close Thera and Crete lie to each other, they thought that at last they had found the explanation of the disaster. They believed that great tidal waves had raced across the sea towards Crete, and earthquakes had followed. Soon afterwards, Crete had been shattered by a violent earthquake. Most of the island — and certainly Knossos — had been reduced to rubble and ruins. Within minutes everything had been wiped out, and the buildings had come crashing to the ground.

So the rule of King Minos was brought to a sharp and violent end.

The photo shows Thera seen from the air. In the centre of the bay are what look like two smaller islands. These are the tops of a great underwater volcano rising above the sea. The water in the bay is so deep that in some places ships anchors don't reach the bottom. The drawing shows how an eruption on Thera affects somewhere as far away as Crete. Tidal waves would spread out swiftly and violently, and smash against the whole Northern coast of Crete

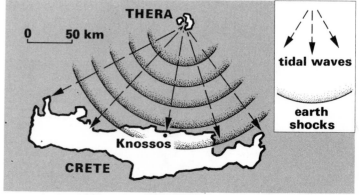

QUESTIONS

See if you can answer these questions. They are all connected with the chapter you have just read. The page number after each question tells you where to find the answer.

1 Who said that Minos was the friend of Zeus? (page 2)
2 How had he learned about Minos and Knossos? (page 3)
3 Why had he not gone to see Knossos for himself? Give two reasons. (page 3)
4 What island near Crete may give us the clue about what happened to Knossos? (page 4)
5 What is this island's other name? (page 4)
6 Certain facts about this island may help us to understand how the Kingdom of Minos was destroyed. What are two of these facts? (page 4)
7 Say briefly what happens when a volcano erupts. (page 6)
8 What is a tidal wave? (page 6)
9 What were two terrible results of the eruption of Krakatoa? (page 7)
10 What really are the two islands in the middle of its bay? (page 8)
11 The water in the bay is very deep in some places. What effect would this have on the tidal waves? (page 8)
12 Why did the eruption of Krakatoa help people to understand how Knossos had been destroyed? (page 8)

THINGS TO DO

1 Make a short list of some volcanoes in the world which still erupt. One of them—in Sicily—is still connected with a Greek god, according to legend. Find out all you can about this—your local library may be able to help you.

Or visit a museum, and see if they have a display about volcanoes: you may be able to see different kinds of lava.

2 Imagine you belong to the crew of a ship which had seen a volcanic eruption. Write a page from the ship's log. Page 6 of Chapter 1 may help you.

3 Draw a picture of a volcano erupting: you might want to show people in a street, trying to escape.

2: THE WORLD OF MINOS

Arthur Evans

Nothing more was known of the Kingdom of Minos until, at the end of the 19th century, an archaeologist called Arthur Evans came to Crete. As a young man, Arthur Evans had been fascinated by Homer's stories. Later he travelled a great deal in Greece to see the places he had read about.

Then he visited Heinrich Schliemann, the archaeologist who had discovered Troy and Mycenae. Schliemann showed Evans tiny carved gemstones: he said that they had been found in Crete. (Stones of this kind were often used to seal boxes or jars—so they were called seal stones. They were also used as magic charms.) Evans was fascinated by their strange markings, which no one could read. He decided to spend time and money finding out what this 'writing' meant. He came first to Crete in 1894. He spent a great deal of money on buying a site at Knossos. With the help of a team of workers Evans began to dig there. The digging went on for almost 30 years. Although he started out by trying to find out about seal stones and their strange markings, he ended up by discovering the Palace of Minos and its treasures.

Seal stones engraved with a mixture of pictures and linear markings (enlarged about three times). Boxes were tied with cords; then the knots were made secure with lumps of clay sealed, or stamped, with the owner's seal. Jar stoppers were also sealed in this way.

What Evans found

Soon after Evans began digging, he found hundreds of clay tablets all lying together, as if they had been carefully stored away. Many were broken, although some were still whole. One is shown in the photograph on this page. The tablets are covered with a kind of sign-writing.

The writing on the tablets tells us a great deal about how the people of King Minos lived. The tablets are records, kept by the king's officials, of the goods which the merchants brought to the Palace, and how much tax his subjects paid. The tablets survived because they were baked hard in the fire which helped to destroy the Palace.

Many more tablets like these, with the same kind of writing, have been found in other places. A great many were found at Mycenae.

A clay tablet found at Knossos

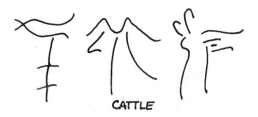

CATTLE

These three examples of sign-writing mean 'cattle'. Can you find them on the tablet?

Frescoes

Evans discovered some other exciting clues about what the people of the Palace had really been like. He found a lot of evidence in the **frescoes** (or wall paintings) in the Palace. Many of these had been almost completely lost when the Palace itself was destroyed. Often, all that was left was a small patch of colour, or the painting of a hand or part of a figure. Evans and the artists who helped him worked with great patience to reconstruct the frescoes —they wanted to make them as they must have looked in the days of King Minos.

Sometimes, tiny bits gave them the clue which they needed, almost as if they were doing a jigsaw puzzle. But they did not always agree about what ought to be put in place of pieces that were missing.

Sometimes archaeologists make mistakes about how a picture or a building should be restored. And because this happens, some people think these should not be restored at all. They think it should be left to us to imagine for ourselves what pictures and buildings once looked like.

As you will see from the next page, some people think that Arthur Evans made a mistake about a fresco.

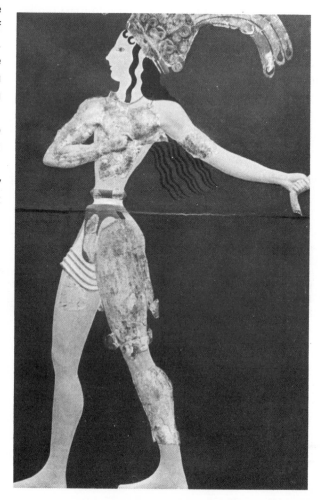

Part of a fresco from the Palace, (partly restored). 2·20 m high

This fresco shows a figure gathering crocuses and putting them into vases. When Evans put the pieces of this painting together, the head was missing. Because he thought the figure was a human being's, he asked his own artist to paint in a boy's head.

But now people think this figure was really a monkey, and should have a monkey's head. If you look carefully above the figure's back, you can see what looks like a tail waving in the air.

The Minoan who originally painted this fresco loved bright colours. He made the figure blue-green, the flowers pale blue, and the background red.

The fresco 'The Saffron gatherer'. Can you spot the bits that have been mended? 25 cm high

Pottery

In the Palace at Knossos Evans discovered many objects made by Minoan potters. He found this little figure in the treasury under the Palace.

The wild goat stands almost as if she were alive: she waits patiently with her head raised, while her two kids feed.

This group is made of **faience**, clay specially treated with a coloured glaze, or coating. The glaze makes the surface glossy, instead of dull.

Minoan craftsmen were skilled in making faience: they used it to make beads and different kinds of small objects.

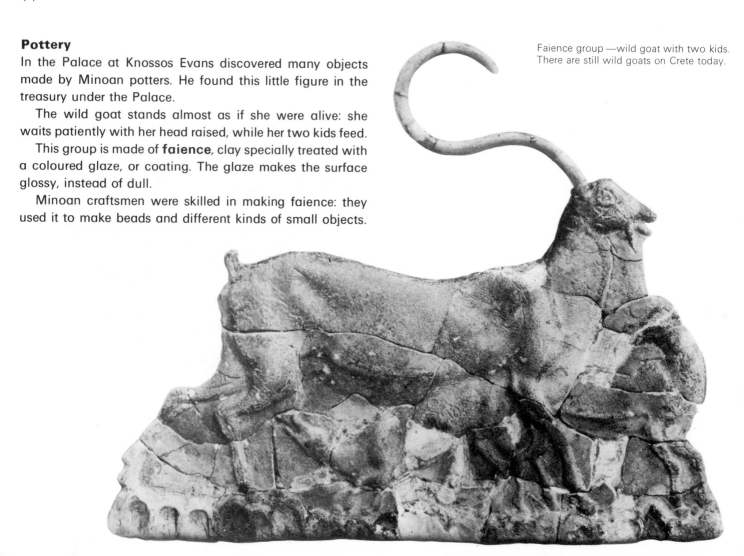

Faience group —wild goat with two kids. There are still wild goats on Crete today.

The vases shown on this page, and the frescoes, show that Minoan artists were skilful and full of imagination. Often they chose flowers and plants for the patterns and designs of their painted vases.

Sometimes the artists chose their subjects from the creatures of the sea round Crete. Fish, dolphins and octopuses must have been well known to the Minoans: all these seem alive on the beautiful vases and jars.

A two-handled flask, painted with a very life-like octopus. When it was found this vase had been shattered into many pieces: it has been carefully put together again. 24·3 cm high

A Minoan vase with a flower decoration. 45·5 cm high

These vases have patterns of plants, fish and birds

The jars in this photograph are usually called by their Greek name, **pithoi**. They are enormous, many of them taller than a man. At Knossos they still stand in rows as they must have done long ago, ready for use. They were made to store great quantities of liquid, wine perhaps or olive oil. Some of them may have been used to contain grain.

They are made of pottery, reddish brown in colour. The handles on them must have been very necessary. You can imagine that it would be difficult, or even impossible, to move jars as big as these if they had no handles. From the number of handles on each jar it looks as if several men would be needed to help with the job.

The Minoan potters made even these everyday jars attractive: they decorated them all with a design of bands and wavy lines.

The Minoans themselves could not possibly have used the great quantities of oil they stored away. They sent much of it overseas to other countries. We know that this happened, for Minoan pottery jars have been found in Greece, Egypt, and Syria.

Huge storage jars stand ready at Knossos beside the pits for storing grain

This *pithos* is decorated with designs of double-headed axes (see page 43) plants and rosettes. 98 cm high

Trade

In their trading ships the Minoans could easily reach Greece and the Greek islands, Egypt and other countries.

In Homer's story, *The Odyssey*, Odysseus pretends to be a Cretan. He says:

We went on board and set sail from the broad land of Crete with the north wind blowing fresh and fair, and ran on as easily as if we were sailing downstream. On the fifth day we came to the fair flowing Nile, and there on the River Nile I anchored my curved ships.

From Egypt the Minoans brought boxes of alabaster (light-coloured stone used for making statues and boxes), and gold jewellery. They brought gold too, for their own craftsmen to use in making gold cups like the one shown on page 22.

From Cyprus they brought copper, and from Syria or Spain, tin. They needed these metals to make their famous bronze weapons.

Map showing countries with which the Minoans traded

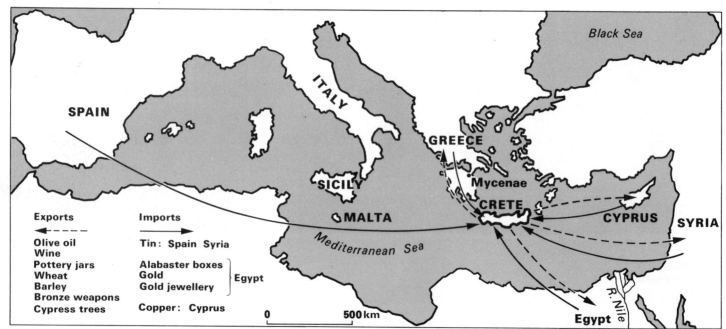

Exports
Olive oil
Wine
Pottery jars
Wheat
Barley
Bronze weapons
Cypress trees

Imports
Tin: Spain Syria
Alabaster boxes
Gold
Gold jewellery } Egypt
Copper: Cyprus

0   500km

The Greek historian Thucydides wrote that 'Minos made himself master of the Greek sea'. Minoan sailors and their great trading ships must have been a familiar and welcome sight in many foreign ports.

Crete is a narrow island. Mountains stretch along it almost without any break. But the land in the plains is fertile, and the Minoans were able to grow good crops of wheat and barley. They could also grow vines and olives easily. All these crops grew so well that the Minoans had far more than they needed for themselves. So they were able to export wheat, barley, wine and olive oil.

Pindar, the Greek poet, called Crete '**polydendron**' — 'rich in trees'. He meant cypress trees, which grow tall and straight. They were good for building ships. Minoan ships often carried cargoes of cypress trees away from Crete.

We know too that foreigners were anxious to buy Minoan weapons. These were designed and made by craftsmen in the Palace workshops. They were famous for their beauty as well as for their strength.

Part of a dagger blade found at Mycenae in Greece, showing men armed with figure-of-eight shields, fighting a lion. It was probably made by a Minoan craftsman. 23·7 cm long

The Minoans were wise enough to know that one way of improving their trade was to be on friendly terms with important foreigners. So they brought gifts to the Pharaoh, the ruler of Egypt. The picture shows them walking in procession, carrying their gifts. One of the men carries a heavy copper ingot on his shoulder. The vases and jugs that they carry look very much like Minoan vases and jugs: the second last figure is carrying a **rhyton**, a jug for pouring *libations* (wine poured out as an offering to the gods).

The Egyptian artist has done his best to paint the strangers in his usual Egyptian style, but he has not succeeded very well. You can see quite clearly that they have long hair. The last man has a long ringlet curling down over his shoulder.

These men were easily recognised by the Egyptians, who had a special name for them. They called them 'men of Keftiu'. Keftiu was the Egyptian name for Crete.

Drawing of an Egyptian tomb fresco, showing Cretans bringing gifts to Pharoah

Craftsmen

Craftsmen are welcome guests from one end of the world to the other.
Homer *Odyssey* Book XVII

This picture shows a Minoan jewel. It is a pendant, made to hang round the neck on a chain, like a necklace.

Two wasps face each other. Above their heads is a cage, with a bead in it. Between them they hold a honeycomb shaped like a gold circle, with tiny dots of gold arranged all over its surface. This is a very difficult way of using gold, but you can see how well the artist has done it here. He has done it successfully on the wasps' eyes and bodies, too. The Egyptians were very skilful at this. An Egyptian may have taught the Minoan artist how to make this pendant. Certainly the Minoan who made this pendant must have been a very good pupil.

The 'wasp' pendant. 4·6 cm high

The Minoans loved jewellery of all kinds, but they specially loved seals. They used them for many different purposes. They used some of them for closing up the necks of jars, or securing knots on cords that tied up chests. We do the same kind of thing today, very often. If the seal is broken before the jar is sold or the parcel arrives, someone has been tampering with it!

Apart from this, people often wore seals because they thought they could give them some kind of magic protection against harm. They wore them as amulets, or lucky charms. Many people who liked to be fashionable wore seals on a cord round the neck, like a pendant. Others preferred to wear them on the wrist, exactly as we wear wrist watches. These seals had a special shape, very much like a lens used in spectacles.

The patterns engraved on the seals were very attractive and sometimes amusing. All kinds of animals and birds were used: so were spiders and octopuses.

At first, soft materials were used — like ivory, which could be shaped and carved with a copper knife. Then, as craftsmen learned how to use drills, they were able to use much harder stones, like amethyst or agate and all kinds of quartz. Specially valuable seals were often made of gold.

This gold cup has been photographed upside down so that you can see the pattern on the underside. The base, on which the cup usually rests, has been left plain. The rest has a pattern of octopuses with their tentacles waving among seaweed. Compare this with the pattern on the vase on page 15

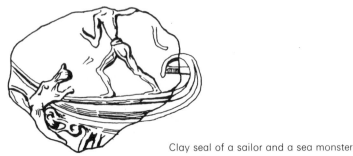

Clay seal of a sailor and a sea monster

More seals

Four cats' heads.
1·7 cm high

Potter at work.
1·3 cm diameter

Spider.
1·3 cm diameter

Hound attacking a wild goat.
1·8 cm diameter

Two people in a chariot.
2·3 cm diameter

Lioness drinking at a fountain.
2·5 cm diameter

QUESTIONS

See if you can answer these questions.

1 Why did Arthur Evans first come to Crete? (page 10)
2 What kind of things did he find soon after he began to dig? (page 11)
3 What two facts do these give us about the people of King Minos? (page 11)
4 In what other place have many more of these been found? (page 11)
5 What is a *fresco*? (page 12)
6 Why was it so difficult for Evans to put frescoes together again? (page 12)
7 Explain briefly what *faience* is. (page 14)
8 What were *pithoi* used for? (page 17)
9 What four things did the Minoans take abroad to sell to other peoples? (page 18)
10 What kind of object specially shows the great skill of Minoan craftsmen? (page 22)
11 Why do you think such great skill was needed for making these? (pages 22, 23)
12 Look at the picture on page 20. What reason would the Cretans have for behaving like this? (page 20)

THINGS TO DO

1 Make a papier-mâché copy of a Minoan vase. Paint it with the kind of pattern which Minoan artists used (page 15).
2 You are a Minoan craftsman. An Egyptian prince has asked you to make him a new dagger.
either
plan your design: make your drawing the size you want the dagger to be,
or
if you prefer writing, write a letter to the prince, explaining what the dagger will be like.
3 Use modelling clay or plasticine to make a copy of one of the clay tablets shown on page 11.

Imagine that it lists ten horses, eight soldiers, four chariots. Invent your own sign-language, and 'write' this list on the tablet. You will need picture signs and number signs. You can get some help from *Mycenae* by Michael Sargent, and *Ancient Crete and Mycenae* by James Bolton (Longman).
4 Imagine that you are Arthur Evans. Write a page from your diary, telling how you found the scattered pieces of the fresco on page 13. Be sure to say how you solved the problem of the piece that could not be found.

3: THE MONSTER AND THE GODDESS

Zeus

On page 2 you read that Minos, King of Crete, was the special friend of Zeus. It's hardly surprising that Zeus was particularly fond of Crete. Legends tell us that when Zeus was newly born, his mother Rhea hid him away for safety in the cave of Dikte on the island of Crete. She was afraid that Kronos, his father, would kill him, out of jealousy. (Kronos had a nasty habit of devouring his own children.) This was one reason why Zeus was particularly fond of Crete.

Bronze figure of Zeus, hurling a thunderbolt. 13.5 cm high

The entrance to the cave of Zeus, on Mt. Dikte. People still come to see the cave where the legends say Zeus was hidden

Many of the Greeks' favourite legends were about Zeus. They loved to hear how Zeus often left his home on Mt. Olympos, and visited men and women on earth. Often he came in disguise. He turned himself into a shower of gold, or a swan, or some other creature. Once he even disguised himself as a bull, and carried off the maiden Europa to Crete, where he married her.

This is how the Greek poet Moschos tells the story of the wedding procession.

Smiling she sat on the back of Zeus the Bull
as he skimmed the vast waves like a dolphin.
The sea grew calm as he sped along
and the Nereids, nymphs of the waters,
rose up from the depths, riding sea monsters.
His brother the Earth-Shaker cleared a path for him over
    the waves and on conch shells the Tritons, musicians
    of the sea, played wedding music.
With one hand Europa gripped the bull's horn
with the other she held the hem of her bright robe
lest it trail in the boundless waters of the white-flecked
    sea, and be wet.
Her robe billowed from her shoulders
like the sail of a ship and supported the girl.

The son of Zeus and Europa was Minos. This was another reason for Zeus being specially fond of Crete.

Zeus and Europa

The monster

Minoan sailors visited strange places, and often met strange people on their travels. When they came home they had exciting tales to tell. Some of these must have been about terrible monsters they had seen. Or so they said! Perhaps the Cretan who made the 'monster' seal on page 22 had been listening to a sailor's story, and got his idea from that. But the Minoans did not have to go far to find a monster. They had one of their own. It was, according to the story, the **Minotaur**, a dreadful creature, half bull, half man. This monster, the Minoans thought, lived below the Palace of King Minos, in a dark **labyrinth** or maze. This labyrinth had been built by Daidalos, who made it so skilfully that no one could ever escape from it. The Minotaur lurked among its dark passages, waiting to pounce on his victims and kill them. No one who entered the labyrinth ever found his way out, but died there, devoured by the monster.

Most stories about monsters have ordinary explanations, and this one has too. If you look at page 41, you will see a plan of the Palace at Knossos. That may explain why people thought that there was a labyrinth below the Palace.

That explains the labyrinth, but what about the Minotaur —the half bull, half man monster? You have read on page 4 that Knossos lay in the centre of an earthquake area. Now earthquakes make a great roaring sound, and it is easy to imagine that people might have thought of the earthquake as a great, roaring bull monster. In fact, when Arthur Evans first came to Knossos, one night there was an earthquake, and he heard a great roaring sound. This is what he wrote:

The building creaked and groaned, and rocked from side to side. A dull sound rose from the ground like the muffled roar of an angry bull.

Coins showing The Labyrinth and the Minotaur

Theseus and the Minotaur

Here is the story of how the Minotaur was killed by the Greek, Theseus, from Athens, in the caves far below the Palace at Knossos.

Once a year the people of Athens had to send seven young men and seven girls to Crete to be fed to the Minotaur. One year Theseus, son of Aigeus, King of Athens, took his place among the young men. He was determined to kill the Minotaur.

When Theseus arrived in Knossos Ariadne, the daughter of Minos, fell in love with him. She found a way of helping him, even though this meant betraying her own father.

She gave Theseus a sword, to kill the Minotaur. Her second gift was a ball of thread. Ariadne told Theseus to fasten one end to the entrance to the Labyrinth, keep hold of the ball, and let the thread out as he walked. After he had killed the Minotaur, he would find his way back to daylight by following the thread.

The plan worked perfectly. Theseus did kill the Minotaur, and came safely out of the Labyrinth.

Athenian women, led by the Goddess Athene, offer gifts to Theseus (from a vase-painting). 17.2 cm high

Theseus tells how he killed the Minotaur.

He stood at bay, against the high wall that carried the stairway above the pit. It was too deep for him to climb out of it except by the steps. I stood at the top of them and called his name. I wanted him to know me. The gold mask turned and the curved eyes faced me. Fixed with that kingly gaze, which lent majesty even to what hid within it, I lifted my arm and gave the salute of the team-leader to the bull.

For a moment he stood with the wall behind him. Then his arm shot out grasping. A shape like a black thunderbolt whirled round him in the air. He had snatched up Mother Labrys from her stand, the King-Eater, the ancient guardian.

I heard his heavy grunting in the hollow mask as he came forward lifting the axe to strike. He had worked round me, to head me off from the steps, and was driving me back against the further wall. I stood up against the wall, and when the axe came at me, dropped like a stone. As it struck the wall where I had been, I seized his leg and threw him. I had time to grab the dagger out of my belt, and drive it home with all the strength left in me. He doubled up with a great cry. I stood up from him, with the axe in my hand. Then I swung Labrys back, and brought her down.

The voice at my feet was silent.

Mary Renault 'The Death of the Minotaur' from *The King Must Die*

Theseus killing the Minotaur (from a vase painting)

You can imagine how delighted Ariadne was to see Theseus coming out of the Labyrinth after killing the Minotaur. The young Athenians must have been overjoyed too. Now they were safe. So were their friends in Athens, safe for ever, thanks to Theseus.

Such a wonderful victory deserved a celebration. The picture on this page shows you the dance that Theseus and Ariadne performed with their friends.

Perhaps this is where the celebration dance took place.

The celebration dance of Theseus and Ariadne

After all this rejoicing you would have expected the story of Theseus and Ariadne to have a happy ending. They sailed away from Crete, on their way to Athens. But Theseus brought his ship to the island of Naxos, and there some kind of magic seems to have taken hold of him. Perhaps some god was jealous, and wished Theseus and his bride no good. Whatever happened, Theseus seems to have forgotten Ariadne, and certainly sailed away without her.

You can imagine Ariadne's feelings as she watched the ship disappearing into the distance. She must have been furious and broken-hearted. And she must have been all the more bitter when she thought that Theseus would never have escaped from the Minotaur if she had not helped him. Probably she had hoped that it would be the will of the gods that Theseus should escape from the Minotaur, and marry her.

The story of how Theseus betrayed Ariadne was never forgotten by the Greeks. They would tell it whenever Ariadne's name was mentioned. If they wanted to tell how a man had completely forgotten someone dear to him, they would say that he forgot 'as men say Theseus forgot Ariadne of the beautiful hair, in Dia'. (Dia is another name for Naxos.)

Theseus and Ariadne boarding an Athenian ship

Perhaps Theseus really had gone against the will of the gods when he left Ariadne. But the Greeks always knew that the gods could not be ignored for very long. As it turned out, Theseus was sailing home to hear terrible news. He had promised his father that he would hoist a white sail on his way home, if he killed the Minotaur. But once again, Theseus forgot. When Aigeus was told that Theseus' ship had been sighted with a black sail, he was so upset that he jumped into the sea and drowned. The gods had punished Theseus after all.

And in the end, the gods had pity on Ariadne. Apollonios of Rhodes tells us how the gods made sure her name would be remembered.

The immortal gods themselves loved her, and in the middle of the heavens they placed a sign, a starry crown. Men call it Ariadne's crown: all night long it rolls along among the heavenly stars.

Apollonios of Rhodes *The Voyage of the Argo*

The Greeks loved this kind of legend, especially when the hero of the story was their own great hero, Theseus. He was their national hero, just as St. George is the great English hero who killed the dragon.

Theseus' ship may have been a black-sailed one like this

The Goddess

The Greeks worshipped Zeus and called him the father of the gods. So they thought of him as head of a whole heavenly family.

But the Minoans seem to have had a very different idea. As far as we can tell they worshipped as their most important ruler a goddess—a female ruler, not a male. You'll notice that all the figures on the ring in the photograph are women. Of course that doesn't mean that men never took part in worship: but it does make us think that women, and especially the goddess, were very much respected.

It's difficult to say exactly what everything on the ring means. For instance, the sun and moon appear together! Beneath the sun and the moon you can see quite clearly a double-headed axe. We know something about this.

The Minoans called it **labrys**. You've seen that name already, in Theseus' story of killing the Minotaur, on page 29. Many drawings and paintings of *labrys* have been found: sometimes it was used as a kind of magic sign which was powerful and mysterious.

Perhaps we can learn something about the goddess. She sits in the open air under a leafy tree. A figure is gathering fruit from the tree: three women are bringing her flowers. Everything round the goddess looks fruitful. She must be a goddess of nature, perhaps the goddess who gives life and fertility to all the earth. Probably she is the great Earth Mother, who was specially important to the Minoans in their worship.

A gold seal ring with goddess and worshippers. 3·4 cm wide

Gold double-headed axe found in a cave. Compare these with the axe shown on page 17

This little statue of a goddess was found under the Palace of Knossos, in the Treasury.

She wears typical Cretan dress of the time, a tight bodice fitting closely into her small waist, and a long flounced skirt, with an apron over it. Everything about her demands respect. She holds a snake in each hand—she is the Snake Goddess. Snakes are creatures of the earth, and so the goddess still has something to do with the earth.

You probably know quite a lot of people who are afraid of snakes. In Britain we mostly see them in zoos: we certainly aren't used to having them as members of the family.

But in the warm climate of Crete the Minoans were quite used to having snakes in their houses. They thought it was lucky to have a snake about: they may even have left out a bowl with food for it, or perhaps milk. They hoped that the snake would guard the house for them, and they were probably glad to encourage it. They may have thought of snakes as pets.

Because of that, it would seem quite natural to them that snakes were kept in special pots, in a special part of the palace, as something holy. And they found nothing strange about worshipping the powerful lady of the snakes, the Goddess herself. It seemed natural to them to ask her to protect the house and everybody in it.

Snake goddess. 29·5 cm high.

QUESTIONS

See if you can answer these questions.

1 Why was Zeus specially fond of Crete? Give two reasons. (pages 25, 26)
2 Who were the *Nereids* and the *Tritons*? (page 26)
3 What was the *Labyrinth*, and why were the Minoans afraid of it? (page 27)
4 Why do you think Theseus was the Greeks' national hero? (pages 27, 28)
5 How did Ariadne help Theseus—and why? (page 28)
6 What was surprising about the way Theseus treated Ariadne? (page 31)
7 Do you think he was punished in some way for this behaviour? (page 32)
8 What kind of proof do we have that the Minoans did not share the Greeks' idea about worshipping a male god? (page 33)
9 What was *labrys*? (page 33)
10 Explain why the main figure on the ring on page 33 is thought to be a goddess of nature. Pick out two main ideas. (page 33)

THINGS TO DO

1 Theseus had many adventures, and the story of them is told on Greek 'black figure' vases. Ask your library if they have any books with pictures of these vases.
2 Read some of the stories about Daidalos, especially the one that tells how Minos chased him after he escaped from Crete. Perhaps your class or school library has a book with these stories in it.
3 Imagine that you are the messenger who brought the news that Theseus' ship was coming home—with a black sail. Write down a report for the new king—Theseus—telling what happened when Aigeus heard your news.
4 Make a model of a maze: use plasticine or card. Put a figure of the Minotaur in the centre of it.
   If you prefer to draw a maze, you could do that. Try to visit a maze. If you live in or near London, Hampton Court or Hatfield House would be a good start. Remember the Minotaur.
5 With the help of one of your friends, act out the killing of the Minotaur. You might write down your dialogue first, or you could make it up as you go along. Perhaps you would prefer to mime—act without using any words at all.

4: THE PALACE OF MINOS

Long ago the Palace of Minos at Knossos was the most magnificent of all the palaces in Crete. Of course a great deal of it was destroyed in the great earthquake and fire. But enough of it is still left for us to see for ourselves what a splendid place it must have been.

You can see from this photograph that hardly anything is left of the upper parts of the palace. Look at the staircase on the right. Now, it leads nowhere: but once it led to the upper storeys of the palace. These storeys have disappeared: the top floors of buildings are the ones which are most quickly destroyed during an earthquake. In any case the pillars which held the ceilings up were made of wood. They would very quickly snap when the earth tremors hit the palace. When they broke, the upper storeys must have collapsed like a pack of cards.

What the Palace of Minos looks like today

This drawing shows us that the palace was a huge place. It was not really a single building at all, but many different ones, joined by corridors and staircases. You can imagine that it would take a visitor a very long time indeed to walk from one end to the other, even if he didn't get lost on the way.

The flat roofs may make you think of some modern building you know—perhaps an office block, or even a school. Most buildings in modern Crete still have flat roofs.

It looks attractive too. But there is one special feature which must have impressed visitors in the time of King Minos. Perhaps they were even a little afraid when they saw this. All along the roof tops, bulls' horns were mounted. These were the royal sign of the power of the King. What's more, when visitors looked at them, they couldn't help thinking about the horrifying tales of the Minotaur.

An artist's picture of what the whole palace might have looked like. It looks surprisingly modern, for such an old building

Sacred horns on the roof tops of the Palace

Here you see part of the west wing of the palace. In the front lies part of the central courtyard: very little is left of the buildings above the courtyard level. In the days of Minos, buildings on this side rose three storeys high. But the Minoan architects had to solve the problem of building on a steep hill. (Look back to page 37.) They managed this by cutting right down into the slope on the eastern side, and cutting part of it away. Then they built *up* to the courtyard level.

Modern architects sometimes do the same thing when they have to design houses to be built on steep slopes. We call these 'split-level' houses.

In the picture you can also see a short flight of steps leading down below the courtyard. Down here were the sanctuary and the crypts or underground cells, lying below the palace, and lit only from tall light shafts.

The west wing of the Palace

Modern split-level housing at Thamesmead, near London

The Palace at Knossos was the largest as well as the most magnificent of all the palaces in Crete.

In the centre of the palace was a huge open courtyard (see the plan on the opposite page). The courtyard was an important place; one reason was that it was used for the bull dance, which you can read about on page 58.

Some people think that the building spread in a muddled way, with no definite pattern. The plan certainly does look like a drawing of a maze.

The palace was a trading centre, government offices, a religious centre and a royal home, all in one. It was cleverly planned round the courtyard in such a way that the different parts were kept separate. The slope of the hill was also used to keep the different parts of the palace separate from each other, so that, for example merchants bringing in their goods to be stored couldn't wander into the royal apartments by mistake.

A famous maze—Hampton Court, near London

Separate entrances

You'll notice that there isn't only one main entrance—as there is at Buckingham Palace. The Palace of Minos had four separate entrances. If you came there in the days of Minos you chose your entrance carefully, depending on your business in the palace.

1 **Main north entrance**
2 **Ramp**
3 **Theatrical area**
4 **Store rooms**
5 **Main east entrance**
6 **Ante room**
7 **Throne room**
8 **Central court**
9 **Shrine**
10 **Grand staircase**
11 **Stone drain**
12 **Hall of the Double Axes**
13 **Main west entrance**
14 **Porch**
15 **Queen's megaron**
16 **Light shaft**
17 **Stone bath**
18 **Main south entrance**

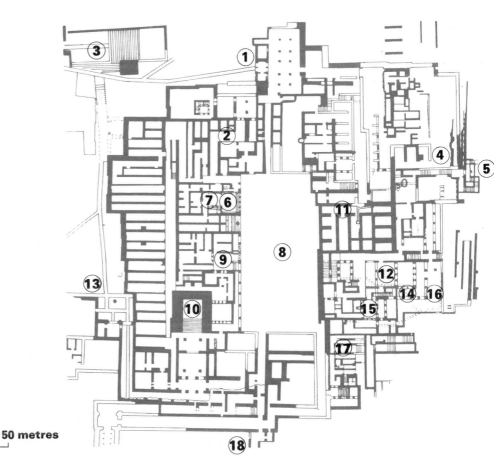

10 5 0   10   20   30   40   50 metres

Here is one of the main entrances to the palace. It lies on the north side: you can see where it is at the top of the plan on page 41.

Important visitors came in by this way, perhaps members of the Court, or foreigners coming to see the King. Once they passed through an entrance gate, they had to go up a slope between the walls to reach the porch above. The architects had made this easier by building a ramp (a paved slope) instead of a flight of steps: this ramp was one of the things which survived the earthquake. But the porch and the wall didn't. Evans carefully rebuilt them.

Look at the pillars which support the roof. Like all the palace pillars they were wooden. Their shape is interesting and unusual. They're wider at the top than at the base. Nobody has thought of a really good reason for this.

You can just catch sight of a fresco on the wall of the porch. Once visitors had come up the ramp into the porch they came face to face with a charging bull. From the photograph you can see how angry it looks. It seems ready to leap off the wall, or attack the tree.

Once visitors were safely past the bull, they reached the open courtyard in the centre of the palace.

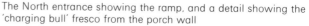

The North entrance showing the ramp, and a detail showing the 'charging bull' fresco from the porch wall

Trading centre

You have already read on page 16 how important oil was to the Minoans. The trading part of the palace must have been one of the busiest parts of the whole building. It was really a great area where the merchants brought their produce to be recorded and stored.

In the photograph the *pithoi* are standing out in the open. But you can see quite clearly that there must once have been walls round them. This was really an underground store: rows of store rooms opened off the long corridor which ran the whole length of the palace.

You can see, too, pits or chests sunk into the floor. Most of these were lined with stone, but some had a lead lining. Probably these were used at first as a kind of underground treasury. Perhaps the pits were used for keeping gold safe, or even specially valuable clothes. Later on, though, they were used as oil vats.

Nowadays banks keep their stores of gold ingots in basement strongrooms. The Minoans too thought that their treasure was safest down below the earth.

People used oil for many different purposes. Homer mentions one in the story where he describes how the Princess Nausikaa and her maids get ready for a picnic.

Nausikaa brought the brightly coloured clothing from the storeroom. She packed it in the polished waggon, and her mother put all kinds of good things to eat in a box. The girl climbed into the cart, and her mother gave her soft olive oil in a golden flask, so that she and her maids could anoint themselves after bathing.

Homer *Odyssey* Book VI

Pithoi in the open

Royal home

On the opposite side of the courtyard from the business part of the palace were the private rooms of the royal family. The ground slopes steeply down the hill on this side. There had to be a staircase leading down to the rooms below the level of the courtyard. And the staircase had to be specially magnificent since it was used by the King and his family.

Here you see the lower part of the staircase. The steps are quite wide and not too steep, easy to go up and down. In the top left corner there is part of an open corridor that looked on to the space in the centre. This is certainly not wasted space. The people who lived in the palace naturally wanted plenty of air and light in the rooms where they lived. But they certainly did not want draughts in winter and baking hot rooms in summer. That's what would have happened if they had had ordinary windows, especially since the Minoans had no window glass. So the architects designed light shafts—rather like modern lift shafts, except that they were open all the way from roof level to the ground.

You get a good idea of how they worked from this photograph. The staircase has plenty of light streaming down from the central courtyard. It would be kept pleasantly cool, with lots of air. But other parts of the building, especially below ground, must have been stuffy and pitch dark.

The main staircase

The Hall of the Double Axes

This great hall is one of the grandest rooms in the palace. It is also the largest, about 12 metres long by 8 wide. Plenty of light flooded into it, for on one side there is a light shaft, and on the other a porch leads to an open terrace. In the photograph you have a view right through to the light shaft. But between each pair of pillars there would have been a set of folding doors. The people inside the room could use these either to keep the room private, or to make it warmer. Light would come in through the sections above the doors.

Arthur Evans called this room the Hall of the Double Axes, because the sign of the double axe had been cut many times into the pillars. He might as easily have called it the King's Room, for he found the remains of a throne here. Probably the King entertained his friends here: he and his men may have used this room when the day's work was finished.

Weapons were often hung on the walls of this kind of room. Sometimes they were for decoration, and sometimes so that they could be snatched up quickly if they were needed. Perhaps you have visited a castle in this country where you've seen this kind of display.

The shields you see in the photograph are copies of the original ones. They give an excellent idea of how impressive the Hall must have been to the King's visitors.

The warrior's great shields were made of as many as seven layers of ox-hide: the top layer was sometimes made of bronze. The whole thing was immensely tough. It could stand the thrust of a spear and not be pierced through.

Here is Homer's description of how a leader of the Minoans, Idomeneos, was saved by his shield:

Deiphobos let fly at Idomeneos with his shining spear. But Idomeneos was watching out, and avoided the bronze spear. He sheltered below his shield which he always carried, a shield of ox-hide and gleaming bronze, like a figure of eight with two rods to hold it. It gave out a dry clang as the spear grazed it and passed over.

Homer *Iliad* Book XIII

A warrior protects himself with his figure of eight shield. It covers the whole of his body except his head and feet. This is from the same dagger as on page 19.

The Queen's apartments

The Queen's **megaron** (main living apartment) was a suite of two rooms. It had all the luxury and richness that you would expect to find in the Queen's private apartments. The main room is attractively decorated: the pillars, the walls, and the ceiling are patterned with rosettes and spirals. Dolphins and fish dart about in the fresco above the door on the left. An inner wall is panelled with frescoes of a Minoan court lady.

Plenty of light and air came into both rooms from two light shafts.

You may be surprised to see that the ladies in the picture have nothing more comfortable to sit on than a stone bench. But there would probably have been wooden stools as well, rather like modern folding stools: these would be used with cushions. Perhaps there was also a tall wooden armchair. None of these have survived: wood rots away and disappears, so do fabrics. However we know from frescoes what the stools were like. You can see one below.

This is an artist's idea of what the Queen's Megaron may have looked like

Skirt of Minoan lady seated on a wooden stool (from a fragment of a fresco)

In this drawing you are looking into the Queen's bathroom. It's as if you had leaned over the low stone wall between the two rooms.

Obviously the bath is the important feature of this room. You'll notice that it has no water pipes leading into it, and no drainpipes. It is a portable bath tub: it was probably carried outside so that the water could be poured away down a drain. The bath measures just over $1\frac{1}{2}$ metres long, big enough for someone to sit in, but not to lie down in comfortably. Maids probably brought water in and poured it over the person in the bath.

Clearly the Minoans were expert plumbers, even though they didn't pipe water into their baths. A fine system of drains carried away rain water from the palace roofs and light shafts. As well as this, water was supplied throughout the whole palace by a system of clay pipes.

You can see one of them on this page. It is designed so that the narrow end fits neatly into the next length of pipe. This helped the water to shoot quickly along the pipes and keep them clear of dirt.

A water pipe from the palace

A Minoan bath tub

Perhaps the Queen used a bath tub like this one. It is decorated on the inside with fish—you can just see two of them under the line painted inside. Outside, it has a pattern of lines and spirals. This looks very much like the kind of pattern you might see on a Cretan lady's skirt—especially the panel on the right hand side (see page 34).

Notice the handles on the outside of the bath. They were fitted to make it easier to move it about, and empty the water down the drain.

In the hot summer of Crete it must have been a real delight—as it is today—to have a bath. Perhaps the Cretans were like the Greeks, and enjoyed a bath especially when they had just finished a long journey—like Odysseus, when he reached the house of Arete, after many days' travelling.

Arete told her maids to set a great three-legged cauldron on the fire as fast as they could. They set the cauldron for bath water on the blazing fire, poured water into it, and brought firewood and kindled it beneath the cauldron. The fire flared up all round the belly of the cauldron, and the water began to heat.

Odysseus was absolutely delighted to see the hot bath water, for he hadn't been used to being looked after like this since he left the home of the beautiful-haired Calypso.

Homer *Odyssey* Book VIII

The most sacred part of the whole palace was the Throne Room. Here is a description of what it looked like when it was discovered by Arthur Evans.

It was found in a state of complete confusion. A great oil jar lay overturned in one corner, ritual vessels were in the act of being used when disaster came.

Everything certainly looked as if some kind of religious ceremony had been violently interrupted.

Unfortunately, nobody in the days of Minos ever wrote down any account of a ceremony in the Throne Room. There isn't even a fresco showing one. Perhaps it was too sacred for a picture of it to be made, or even to be talked about. But probably the King took a leading part in it. He may have sat on his throne, guarded by a griffin on the wall on each side of him. (You can see griffins in the picture—they are imaginary creatures with lion bodies and eagle heads.)

We know that as well as being King, he was also Priest of his people. So he may have been busy pouring out oil from the great storage jar as an offering to the Earth Goddess. Or he may have gone down the short flight of steps to the underground room. The Minoans probably believed that when he went down into the earth he came close to the Earth Goddess. The King may have hoped that she would give him extra power to prevent disaster.

Reconstruction of the King's throne from the Hall of the Double Axes

The Throne Room of the King as it looks today

QUESTIONS

See if you can answer these questions.

1 What parts of the Palace of Knossos were most quickly destroyed when the earthquake happened—and why? (page 36)

2 What sign was used all along the Palace rooftops? What would it probably make visitors think of? (page 38)

3 How did the Minoan architects get round the problem of building on a steep slope? (page 39)

4 The Palace was the King's home. Apart from that, what two other uses did it have? (page 40)

5 What two sorts of things may have been kept in the storage pits? What certainly was kept there? (page 43)

6 How did the Minoans make sure that plenty of light and air reached the main rooms in the Palace? (page 44)

7 What is there in the Queen's apartments that might show us that the Minoans liked to live in a civilised way? (page 48)

8 What special responsibility did Minos have as well as being King? (page 50)

9 On the last day at Knossos why should the Minoans have wanted their King to offer worship to the Earth Goddess? (page 50)

THINGS TO DO

1 Draw or paint a picture of the Palace at Knossos—remember the sign on the roof tops.

2 Write the 'lost' account of the last hours in the Throne Room as the earthquake struck. Imagine that you are one of the King's own men who somehow managed to escape.

3 Make a papier-mâché model of a Minoan warrior complete with his figure of eight shield, and his spear. Use thin card or balsa wood for his shield: cut out scraps of leather for the covering, and use metal foil for the shield boss.

or

Work with a few friends and make a full size figure of eight shield for one of your group. Cut the shapes for the shield from heavy card, or cardboard boxes: mount them on two wooden strips—read page 46. Make the covering of thin card or cloth, painted reddish brown. Cut the top layer from metal foil.

4 Try to find out how modern architects let light into rooms or corridors where windows can't be used. (Think about the kind of material that can be used instead of solid brick.)

5: THE BULL AND THE MINOANS

A crowd waiting for the game to begin in the central courtyard (from a fresco)

The Minoans were always being reminded of the power of the bull —by the bull's horns, the bull fresco, and the story of the Minotaur. It's hardly surprising that their favourite sport was bull leaping.

You can see from this fresco how they came in their hundreds to watch. Tiers of seats, like a grandstand, were put up in the central courtyard on each side of the shrine. It looks as if everybody in Knossos is celebrating a public holiday. Most people have come in good time for the show, for every seat is occupied. Some have arrived too late to get a seat. You can see them standing at the sides. Some of them are looking along the rows, perhaps still hoping to find a seat. Others seem to have given up that idea. They have turned away, perhaps to watch for a sign that something is going to happen at last.

The fashionable ladies in the front seats have the best place of all. But they are deep in conversation, almost as if that was really why they had come. Only one of them looks as if she had something else to think of. She has raised her hand, as if in salute. Perhaps she has seen the King arriving.

The audience

Here are some of the Court ladies from the audience. They are dressed in the height of fashion. They have taken a great deal of time and trouble on their appearance.

Their hair is elaborately styled with curls carefully arranged on the forehead, and a specially long curl down the side of the face. They seem to have emptied their jewel boxes for the occasion. Besides wearing necklaces and bracelets all of them wear jewelled head-dresses and have tied back their plaits with jewelled bands.

Their clothes are smart too, brightly coloured dresses with puffed sleeves, cleverly cut bodices open at the front and fitting tightly into the waist, and long flared skirts, heavily patterned in bands. The designers of these clothes must have been very skilful, so must the workers who sewed and embroidered them.

These may be special clothes for a special occasion. Court ladies may have been expected to wear a particular style of dress when they were on duty. Probably they wore simpler clothes for everyday use. Women who had to work in the fields would certainly wear plainer clothes, easier for working in (see page 33).

Ladies of the court (from a fresco)

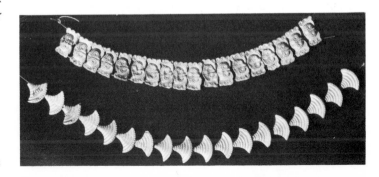

Some fine gold necklaces

The Bull Leapers

This picture shows one of the most exciting moments of the bull game. Three leapers are busy, two girls and a man. The man has just somersaulted over the bull's horns on to the middle of its back. In a moment he will leap off backwards to land on the ground behind the bull. There he will be steadied by the assistant who waits, slightly to one side, on tiptoe with hands outstretched to help him.

The bull-leaping fresco

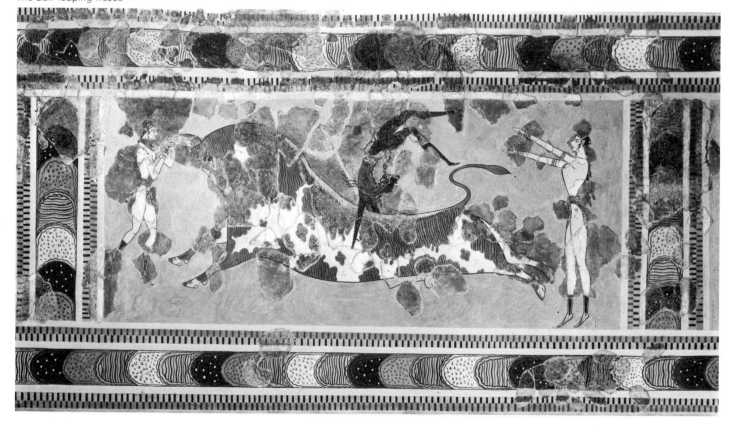

The double somersault was extremely dangerous. You can see how immensely powerful this bull must have been. He looks enormous compared with the slender leapers. His great neck is arched like a powerful spring, ready to shoot up and back and toss the leaper high into the air.

The girl who grasps his horns is not trying to hold him back. She will be next to leap, so she is getting her grip right. She is almost ready to lever herself up over the horns, land on his back, and vault off again.

Quite clearly, the leapers are unarmed. This is because they are really members of a team of acrobats. They depend on each others' skill to turn away the bull's attention if he catches them off their guard and corners them.

They had no intention of killing the bull. But a leaper had only to make a single slip or lose his concentration for a single second. Then the bull would charge, and that would be the end of the bull leaper.

Bronze statue of a Cretan bull and leaper. 11·1 cm high

Seal stone showing a bull and leaper. 1·7 cm diameter

This little figure of a bull leaper is carved from ivory. Perhaps he was one of a group of figures, including the bull himself. This leaper is in the act of leaping over the bull's back. His whole body is beautifully balanced and perfectly controlled, from his outstretched hands to his toes.

The next time you watch a good gymnast swinging on parallel bars, compare him with this leaper. You'll see how the gymnast controls every muscle, too.

The diagram shows you the stages of the leap. It would take only a few seconds from start to finish.

Ivory figure of a single bull leaper (in act of leaping). 24.5 cm high

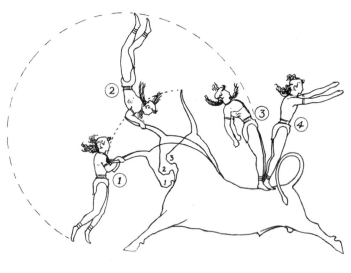

Bull-leaping as a sport still goes on in France today. The man in this photograph is French, not Minoan, and he lives in France. But any Minoan would recognise at once what he is doing, and admire his skill and courage. (Compare him with the leaper on page 55.)

Notice that the animal is held on a rope, but it can still move very fast, and charge violently. The leaper can't afford to make a single slip.

This leaper is taking as many risks as the Minoan leapers did. And the French audience have something in common with the Cretan audience, too, for they are watching the game from behind a safety barrier!

Modern French bull-leaper

This is a wine-pourer, or *rhyton*, used for pouring offerings of wine or blood to the gods. It is in the shape of a bull's head. It was made in Crete in the time of King Minos

The Bull Dance

A trumpet sounded. In the wall facing us the great bull-gate opened, and out ran the bull. He was a kingly beast, thick-barrelled, short-legged, wide-browed, and very long horned. The Corinthian stood facing him across the ring. I saw him lift his hand, saluting: a noble gesture, graceful and brave. Then the dancers began to move round the bull, turning in a circle as the stars do round the earth. The music quickened and the dancers closed in. They swooped round the bull like a flight of swallows, nearer and nearer. Now the dancers slowed their spinning and started to play the bull. First one and then another would pause until they had drawn him, then skim out of his path and leave him for the next. The more daring the dancers are, the more they work the bull, the better for them in the end. He may tire first, if they keep him at it. Then the Corinthian ran round to face him, and held out both arms; the circling stopped. He ran smoothly up to the sullen bull. He grasped the horns, and swung up between them, going with the bull: then he soared free. He turned in air, a curve as lovely as a bent bow's, and on the broad back his slim feet touched down together: then they sprang up again. He seemed not to leap, but to hang above the bull, like a dragon fly over the reeds, while it ran out from under him.

Then he came down to earth, feet still together, and lightly touched the catcher's hands, like a civility: he had no need of staying. Then he danced away.

Mary Renault *The King Must Die*

The man in this fresco is obviously very important. He is dressed in a pair of cut-away trunks like the ones the bull leapers wore. He is broad-shouldered and narrow-waisted: he has the kind of splendid figure which the Minoans admired so much.

The artist who created this fresco seems to have taken special care to make the figure in it impressive, perhaps because it shows a very special person, on an important occasion. His long hair flows down his back, and lies across his forehead in carefully dressed ringlets, with a long tendril curving down his ear. He wears a fine jewelled collar for this occasion. His left arm is stretched out as if he were leading an animal by the rope he holds in his hand.

But the most striking thing about him is his headdress. It is an elaborate one, with splendid plumes arching out from the top of it. He seems to be taking part in a procession: perhaps he is leading a sacred animal, to make offerings at a sanctuary in the palace.

Many people think that he really is someone very important indeed to the Minoans—their Priest King.

The Prince of the Lilies—from a restored fresco

The end of the Bull

These bull games were very special to the Cretans. They were really more than a sport. The Cretans were fascinated by the bull and his great power. The bull was also the special creature of the Earth Goddess. They may have believed that the Goddess kept a great bull beneath the earth: from time to time she would let it go free, to cause destruction. Then the earth would rumble and shake, and buildings would fall to the ground as he roared in fury.

So the Minoans may have felt that the right thing to do at the end of the bull leaping, was to sacrifice the bull to the Goddess. Probably the King himself slew the animal, once it had been bound and dragged before him. This picture shows a bull trussed and waiting to be sacrificed. A priestess puts her hands on the altar in front of a great double axe. (Notice the pairs of horns at the far side).

Once the bull was killed, its blood may have been poured out in a libation from a **rhyton** like the one on this page.

A bull's head *rhyton*

Fresco showing a sacrificial scene, with a bull trussed ready for slaughter

'Minos, glorious son of Zeus'

If you had to pick out a word which is used a great deal in this book, you'd probably pick out 'Minoan'. That's not surprising, since Minos gave his name to his own kingdom; quite naturally, his own people and the time in which they lived were called after this powerful king. He passed on his name to the rulers of Crete who came after him, too. They used the name 'Minos' as a title, just as all Egyptian rulers were called Pharaoh.

So although Minos and his kingdom disappeared, his name lived on.

As you've seen, the Greeks always remembered Minos because of Homer's words about Crete (page 1). But there was another reason. When Odysseus visited the World of the Dead, which the Greeks called Hades, this is what he said he saw there.

Coin showing head of Minos. 32 mm diameter

There I saw Minos, glorious son of Zeus, sitting with his golden sceptre in his hand, judging the dead. And they sat and stood all round the King throughout the house of Hades with its wide gates, and asked him for judgment.

Homer *Odyssey* Book XI

The earthly kingdom of Minos had been destroyed, but as every Greek believed, he was still powerful, in the Kingdom of Hades.

QUESTIONS

See if you can answer these questions.

1 What seems to have been the Minoans' favourite entertainment? (page 52) Where did it take place? (page 52)

2 Very briefly describe the dress of the ladies of the Minoan Court. (page 53)

3 Do you think it likely that they dressed like this every day? (page 53)

4 What is one of the surprising things about the people who made up the bull team, especially since their job was very dangerous? (page 55)

5 Why was the double somersault so dangerous? (page 55)

6 Where in the world does something very like the Minoan bull leaping take place? (page 57)

7 In what way does this very much resemble the Minoan sport? (page 57)

8 Did the Minoans think of this only as a sport? (page 60)

9 What special ideas did they have about the bull? (page 60)

10 How would this help to explain to a Minoan why Knossos was destroyed? (page 60)

11 What connection may the bull's head have had with the Earth Goddess? (page 60)

12 How—and why—did the Greeks believe that Minos was more powerful than ever, after his death? (page 61)

THINGS TO DO

1 Make a drawing of the scene in the central courtyard on a bull game day. Include the splendid young man shown on page 59, as well as some of the Court ladies.

2 Odysseus' story about his visit to Hades (page 61) stops before he says anything about what kind of judgment Minos gave. Imagine that Odysseus saw Theseus (pages 28–32) coming to Minos. Write down what happened. Don't forget that Minos must reward or punish Theseus.

3 Make a papier-mâché model of a bull—like the one in the picture on page 54. You could make a model of a leaper who has landed on the bull's back. (Use a match sharpened at both ends, to keep the leaper steady.) Or imagine that you are a Cretan, and have just watched the bull dance in the Palace courtyard. Write down your story of what you saw. Write as if you were writing a report for your local newspaper.

4 Bull games are popular in Spain, the Basque country, and France. See if your school library has any books about this. If not, ask at your local public library.

IMPORTANT PEOPLE AND EVENTS

Minoan civilisation at its height

BC	Crete	Greece	Asia Minor	Egypt	Britain
2000	Cretan ships ruled the sea				Stonehenge— building started
1600		Mycenae: Kings buried in *shaft graves* (deep oblong trenches) in the royal Grave Circle			Stonehenge finished: dagger thought to be Mycenean carved on bluestone circle at Stonehenge Bronze Age
1500	Knossos destroyed sometime during this period	Theseus lived (the date is very uncertain)			
1400	Kingdom of Minos ends	Thera erupted		Tutankhamun	
1200		Agamemnon (King of Mycenae) Menelaos (King of Sparta and brother of Agamemnon)	Trojan War		
	Idomeneos (son of one of kings of Crete)		Deiphobus (son of Priam, King of Troy)		
800		Homer . . . the *Iliad* and the *Odyssey*			

BOOKS TO READ

In the *Iliad*, Homer's story of the Trojan War, Homer tells how the men of Crete came to the help of the Greek King Menelaos and how they sailed to Troy and fought there along with the Mycenaeans and other Greeks.

You can read an account of the bull-dance in *Modern Stories of Ancient Greece*, published by Longman. This account comes from the story of Theseus' Cretan adventure, *The King Must Die*, by Mary Renault, also published by Longman. Other books to read are *Men and Gods* by Rex Warner, *The Trojan War* by Wormald, *Mycenae* by M. Sargent, *The Odyssey of Homer* by Wormald, and *Odysseus Returns* by K. McLeish (the last four books are all published by Longman). Legends about Zeus, and Theseus, are told in *Myths of Ancient Greece* by Emile Genest, published by Burke, and in *The Picture Book of Greek Mythology* by Richard Patrick, published by Octopus.

Other books about Crete include *Ancient Crete and Mycenae* by James Bolton (in the Longman 'Then and There' series) and *Crete* in the Bodley Head series on archaeology.

Lion Gate and Labyrinth by Hans Baumann also tells the story of how Knossos was excavated. This book has many pictures.

Larger, highly illustrated books that may help with projects are:

The Home of the Heroes, by Sinclair Hood, published by Thames and Hudson.

Minoan Crete by H. E. Mellersh, published by Evans.

The Buildings of Ancient Greece by Helen and Richard Leacroft, published by Brockhampton.